Heating & Cooling

Heating & Cooling

52 MICRO-MEMOIRS

BETH ANN FENNELLY

W. W. NORTON & COMPANY

Independent Publishers Since 1923

NEW YORK | LONDON

Copyright © 2017 by Beth Ann Fennelly

For information about permission to reproduce
selections from this book, write to Permissions,
W. W. Norton & Company, Inc., 500 Fifth Avenue,
New York, NY 10110

For information about special discounts for bulk
purchases, please contact W. W. Norton Special Sales at
specialsales@wwnorton.com or 800-233-4830

Manufacturing by Quad Graphics Fairfield
Book design by Ellen Cipriano
Production manager: Lauren Abbate

ISBN 978-0-393-60947-9

W. W. Norton & Company, Inc.,
500 Fifth Avenue, New York, N.Y. 10110
www.wwnorton.com

W. W. Norton & Company Ltd.,
15 Carlisle Street, London W1D 3BS

1 2 3 4 5 6 7 8 9 0

For Tommy, provider of the married love—
and in memory of his father,
Gerald Franklin,
1933–2016

CONTENTS

Heating & Cooling

In every book my husband's written, a character named Colin suffers a horrible death. This is because my boyfriend before I met my husband was named Colin. In addition to being named Colin, he was Scottish, and an architect. So you understand my husband's feelings of inadequacy. My husband cannot build a tall building of many stories. He can only build *a* story, and then push Colin out of it.

ONE DOESN'T ALWAYS WISH TO CONVERSE ON AIRPLANES

but this tanned, fit couple—white-sweatered, like tennis pros—seemed eager to talk, so we talked. No, their final destination wasn't Denver. They'd continue to Hawaii after the layover. How awesome, I said, Hawaii. Is it a special occasion, an anniversary? They grinned at each other, like *You tell her. No, you.*

Their thing, it turned out, was scuba diving with metal detectors. They dove at popular honeymoon spots on Oahu, because, they said, the first time those rich Japanese brides hit the water, their new diamonds slid right off. The couple said they didn't always find a ring, but overall they'd found enough to fund their vacations.

"That's . . . wow," I said.

They grinned at each other again, and took a sip from their Bloody Marys, then she gave his biceps a squeeze. Her diamond ring broadcast sequins of light on the tray table. I envisioned how, after netting a big rock, they'd perform exceedingly athletic hotel sex. Their avarice was so unabashed that it was difficult to keep despising them, but I, large of righteousness and small of diamond, persevered all the way to Denver.

I peaked early, fourth grade. I had the lead in *Mary Poppins*. Mr. Banks was played by Vince Vaughn. Yes, *that* Vince Vaughn, though at that point he was nobody, just another kid like the rest of us. He didn't go to Hollywood until after high school.

I don't particularly recall him as being the one destined for stardom.

And what is it you do? he asked, after a moment of silence. My mother was in the bathroom exchanging her dress for the cotton gown.

I had the sense that he was asking to fulfill some kind of med school training: *Engage the patient's loved ones in conversation.*

Five outlandish occupations pinged through my head, all lies. But I knew I shouldn't mess with him. I needed to get him on our side and keep him there. *I'm a writer,* I said.

A rider? A light turned on in his eyes, suddenly as blue as his scrubs. He put his fists up and bounced them: a cowboy bounding over the plains.

No, I said. *A writer.* Which now seemed to require a gesture, so I held up my imaginary pen and wiggled it.

Oh, he said, all business again as my mother came out of the bathroom. *Well,* he said, *me too.* He untied her gown with one hand and slipped the black Sharpie from his pocket with the other, clamped it between his teeth to remove the cap, then drew dashes on my mother's naked chest, indicating where his scalpel would go.

That Friday, after morning Mass, the priests visited our third grade to announce a meeting for prospective altar boys.

I went. Me, Beth Ann. Why did I go? First, I was attracted to the pageantry: the costuming with the alb and the cincture, the procession with the cross and the thurible filled with incense. I wanted to arrange the credence table—the corporal, the cruet, and the ciborium. I wanted to raise the aspersorium of holy water into which the priest dipped the aspergillum before raining blessings on penitent heads. When he lifted the Eucharist, I wanted to twist the cluster of brass sanctus bells, alerting our souls to transubstantiation, bread and wine miracled into Body and Blood. And clearly I wanted to fill the chalice of my mouth with the wine of those words.

Also, I went to prove a point.

But I never got the chance. Before the meeting began, Father Mayer evicted me from the front pew. "I'll be right back," he told my classmates, then steered me by my shoulder to the sacristy where, behind a heavy door, a few old ladies bent over ironing boards. *The altar society,* he informed me, *cares for the priestly vestments. This is where God calls you to serve.* He fled, and I fled, and that evening in my best penmanship I tattled on him to Cardinal Joseph Bernadin. My letter ended, *P.S.: And women should be priests!* My mom loved the letter: how cute, our little women's libber.

Now, a grown woman with children of my own, back in Illinois at my mother's table, I read in *The Trib* that Father Mayer sexually abused altar boys. For decades. He'd been removed from St. Mary's and sent to St. Edna's, removed from St. Edna's and sent to St. Stephen's, removed from St. Stephen's and sent to St. Dionysius', removed from St. Dionysius' and sent to St. Odilo's. All those altered boys. Did the archdiocese, the Cardinal, know? *Please.* In the church files, there's a contract Father Mayer signed, promising that at St. Odilo's he wouldn't be alone with boys under twenty-one. Because by then two of his altar boys had committed suicide.

After St. Odilo's, he was sent to jail.

You can look all of this up, if you care to. Father Robert E. Mayer, pastor of St. Mary's, Lake Forest, Illinois, 1975 to 1981. Call this fiction: I dare you.

I lay the newspaper down in a light that is no longer the light of my mother's kitchen, but is the stained light of St. Mary's, where solid pillars of dust propped up the clerestory windows. In this light I see it all anew, I see it all anew, and clear as a bell, as we say, as if cued by altar boys twisting the sanctus bells, announcing that something has been transubstantiated into something else, forever. The ironing women who lifted the blank communion wafers of their faces. The click of dress shoes as Father rushed back to the meeting, his robes streaming behind him like wings. A year later, his sabbatical. His goodbye pot-luck.

My outrage at not being chosen. My bad luck at being born a girl.

My classmate Donny O'Dell, who *was* chosen, during Mass that unseasonably warm Easter—he was holding high the Bible, rigid and dutiful, when suddenly he toppled backward. The whole congregation heard the sickening thwack of skull on marble, and as one, we uttered the same surprised *Oh!*—as if it were part of the Mass, as if a response had been inserted before the Agnus Dei— *Oh!* we cried, in a single voice—and how quickly Father was at his side, bending, lifting in his arms the small boy, Donny O'Dell, a boy even smaller than I was, Donny in his arms like Jesus removed from his cross, or, with his white alb flowing toward the floor, like a bride. And how Donny raised a hand to his head and opened his eyes and realized that he'd fainted and smiled sheepishly. How the parishioners laughed a relieved laugh to see he was okay. How the ushers led Donny outside into the fresh air. How later, filing out into the narthex, everyone laughed again with Mrs. O'Dell. *Your son gave us quite a scare, Nance. For a moment, we thought he was a goner.*

I COME FROM A LONG LINE
OF MODEST ACHIEVERS

I'm fond of recalling how my mother is fond of recalling how my great-grandfather was the very first person to walk across the Brooklyn Bridge on the second day.

Once, when we were young and poor, my husband and I learned that an Irish friend was road-tripping across America with two Irish pals, so we invited them for a visit. They arrived sniping at one another. They'd had a falling out, and in fact after dinner they were to have a doozy in our driveway that stopped just short of fisticuffs, then go their separate ways. But, before this happened, when thanking us for the meal, one of the men opened his wallet and held out a fifty-dollar bill. Don't be silly, we said, we're not taking your money. He insisted. Thanks, we said, but no. He kept at it, clutching the bill. The more we rejected his money, the angrier he got. Finally, we accepted it. All I could figure is that he had plenty of dough, and felt bad that the three of them had argued, and wanted to make up something to someone, somehow.

Perhaps if we'd acquired the fifty through some usual channel, we'd have stored it in some usual place. But it wasn't paycheck money, it was found money. My husband walked to the bookshelf, opened a book to its fiftieth page, slotted the bill there, then slid the book back. That way we could kind of forget about it, but we'd have it for an emergency: an elegant solution.

We were poor and young, I already said that, and

dumb with love. One night, I was working at my desk when my husband wanted to frolic. He called for me and I delayed, needing ten minutes to finish my project, then ten more. Finally I heard a noise and looked up. He wasn't there, but his penis was, jutting from the doorframe. Out of sight, he gyrated so his penis beckoned, like a crooking finger, and we both got the giggles. My camera was on my desk, and, still giggling, I took a photo, then followed him into the bedroom where we made our love.

Weeks later, when I picked up the developed film, it took me a minute to recall why I'd photographed my door. But oh, there it was: my husband's penis. I showed him, and together we laughed. Then he moved to tear it up, but I stayed his hand. Let me keep it, I argued. Let me keep it someplace secret.

Into a book, page fifty.

It couldn't have been more than a few months later when we found ourselves desperate for dough. We walked to the shelf and removed the book in the upper left corner, turned to page fifty. No money. We opened the next book, the next. No money. We'd neglected to note which book contained the money, but knew where to look, forgetting that we tend to dip frequently into favorites, then reshelve them in the nearest space. We expanded our search. No fifty anywhere. And then I remembered the penis. Now we were searching for both. We checked the fiftieth page of every book in our house constructed of books.

We must have loaned them out. We do that, we can't help it. We collect strays, lost students who need some pals, some protein, and sooner or later we're incredulous, "But you've never read Hopkins?" or "You'd adore Denis Johnson," and a few hours later the student is saying good-bye with a doggie bag and an armload of inspiration. But we couldn't remember any recent borrowers, and couldn't imagine asking about the bonus material, even if we had. Did we lend both books to the same student? If so, in what order? Fifty then penis, we decided, was slightly less salacious than penis followed by fifty.

It's been nineteen years. Our house has more books than ever: not just poetry and fiction and memoir, but biographies, cookbooks, thrillers, graphic novels, mysteries. I love a good mystery. Like, where the hell is that photo? Even now, middle-class and middle-age, I never open a book without hoping for a fifty or a penis.

MOMMY WANTS A GLASS OF CHARDONNAY

If you collected all the drops of days I've spent singing "Row, row, row your boat" to children fighting sleep, you'd have an ocean deep enough to drown them many times over.

Watch what you say about younger sisters within older sisters' earshot. You know, things like, "What beautiful curls the little one has! And what long eyelashes!"

Forty years later I can still feel the yank on my scalp as my four-year-old sister pulled my curls so she could shear them. Can still feel, as I sat trapped by the high chair's embrace, her finger forcing my eyelid down. Can still hear the scissors' *snick, snick.*

Funny, but what I wonder at now is not that she did it, but that when I realized she was going to do it, I didn't struggle. She was going to do it whether I liked it or not, so I sat still. Even then, I had an instinct for self-preservation. And you see, I was right. I am alive, and she isn't.

I WAS NOT GOING TO BE YOUR TYPICAL

mother of a teenager   lament my daughter   my daughter's
friends bodiless as car horns   indistinguishable
as fine airborne particles   of filed fingernails   yet
you saunter through the door   your
Styrofoam Sonic cup   long as your femur   no one
is who you hung out with   nothing is what you talked about
you   speed-inserter-of-the-ear-buds
filching my favorite sweater   which almost flatters me
until you explain   "tomorrow is 80s day at school"   I know

you don't want to hear me   reminisce   about the years
in which I fed you   from my body   how
nearly naked on my naked chest   you'd scrunch-smell
toward my milk   blind and earnest   as a worm   drunk years

those were drunk years   yet even after those drunk years
there were   years in which your every bite   was proffered
from my hand   jar   of pureed peaches snug in my palm
pop of lid   tink   of rubber-coated spoon
every third bite scooped   from your fat cheeks   deposited
back on the pillow of your tongue   until   all done

my two-note song   all done   your face
a messy plate   I could lick clean   you

never had bad breath in those days   not even
in the mornings   peaches, yes,   but   sometimes
even with green beans   I'd lick you clean

WHY I'M SWITCHING SALONS

"We can put on a topcoat with glitter," said the manicurist. "We've noticed you like attention."

We didn't question. Or complain. It wouldn't have occurred to us, and it wouldn't have helped. I was eight. Julie was ten.

We didn't yet know that this blizzard would earn itself a moniker that would be silk-screened on T-shirts. We would own such a shirt, which extended its tenure in our house as a rag for polishing silver.

So I didn't make up the blizzard, though it sounds made up, the grimmest of Grimms, wind chill forty below, three feet of snow and snow still falling. Later, a neighbor would tell of coming home after two nights away and having to dig down a foot to reach his keyhole.

My dad had a snow blower, which spewed sheets of snow out the side of its mouth. Sheets became walls reaching almost to the sky on either side of our front path. By tipping my head back, I could still view sky. It was snow-white and tearing itself into pieces and hurling them at us.

And then the world began shutting down. The airports, which was bad because Mom was in Toronto, visiting her sister. The schools, which was great for the first day, and good for the second, and then less good and less good yet. Because the roads were narrowing, the fridge emptying. Does this smell okay to you? Couldn't watch *Little House* because Channel 5 only covered the blizzard. A motorist, dead of exposure in a stranded car. A snow shoveler, dead of a heart attack, ambulance couldn't reach him. Coat drive, shelters for the homeless. Check in on your elderly neighbors, folks. If you can get out, that is. Amtrak trains abandoned like last year's toys. Cars lining the highway, buried by snow, white lumps pierced by antennas. Family of five, killed when their roof collapsed. We were a family of four, but with Mom away, we were three. I got out of the bathtub to answer her crackling long-distance call.

Then it was Sunday so Dad said get ready for Mass. We didn't question. He helped us tug and wriggle into our snow suits and we slid our feet into plastic bread bags before yanking on our boots. He shouldered open the door into the shrieking tunnel of white. We trudged between walls of snow to the unplowed road. Follow me, Dad said, step where I'm stepping, this part will hold our weight. Except sometimes we couldn't match his stride or it wouldn't hold our weight and Julie's boot or my boot would crunch through crust and we'd plummet to the groin, feeling nothing below but more snow. On the count of three, Dad said, and hoisted us out, and we battled on, snow melting into our socks, heads lowered against the wind. When we reached the plowed road, we scrabbled down, easier walking. I couldn't tell how far we had to go. It hurt to look up.

At last, the dark church loomed. We climbed the stone steps to the doors. Locked. My father raised his gloved fist and knocked. He must have known, even as he knocked, but still he knocked. No sign on the door announced that Mass was canceled. But why should the priests post a sign? Probably they couldn't get out of the rectory themselves.

Right-e-o, said my father, slowly turning back the way we'd come. *Right-e-o*. Whatever he felt then, gazing out over the tundra, the alien tundra, all mailboxes and road signs and newspaper racks and parking meters blighted and buried, wasn't something he shared. What he shared was, *Home again, home again, jiggety jig*.

We descended the steps, back into the scouring wind. Where was everybody? Elderly couple, found in their basement, dead of hypothermia. Fourteen-year-old boy poisoned by carbon monoxide in a running car his dad was digging from a snow bank. Another shoveler's heart attack. Volunteers with snowmobiles taking doctors to hospitals.

Every part of my body was scalding cold, but one part scalded coldest: my neck, my plump child's neck. The wind was wily, cupping my lowered chin and arrowing along the inch of skin before my parka's zipper. The wind, like a squirrel wielding knives. How much farther? I tried to step where he was stepping. I tried to block the wind with his body. Family of three or four, frozen dead on the road, hadn't gone to Mass. Which was a sin. When sinners died, they went to hell.

Finally, I did it, what I'd been contemplating for the last half mile. I shouted at my dad's back, asking for his scarf. I didn't want to ask. I wasn't a child who asked. And I knew he must be cold, too. Yet I asked, and when I did, he turned, already unwrapping his red and black striped scarf. He squatted and tied it around my neck, he wound it once, he wound it twice, he wound it three times, he smiled at me, his handsome Black Irish smile, and behind his scarf, which covered my neck all the way to the tip of my nose, I smiled, too. And thought that I might make it, after all.

Why are people nervous to become parents? Children are so accepting. So stupid. For years—would you believe it?—for years, I'd think of this as a happy memory, my father snugging his scarf around my neck.

But gradually I corrected myself. First, I overheard the late-night argument, the barb about Dad dragging us to church in a blizzard. And in time I recognized the catholicism of rigidity, the Victorian strictures of our house. And eventually I realized that if he were to footslog us over two miles round-trip at nineteen degrees below, he sure as shit should have dressed us in scarves.

And so, with each time my thoughts are blown back to the Blizzard of Seventy-Nine, I unwind that scarf, unwind its loops around my neck. With my self-pity I unwind it; with my self-righteousness I unwind it; even with my care while dressing my own soft children, I unwind it, the very care I take (*Here are your mittens, kitten, here your warmest socks*) a reprimand of him, and then the scarf is off my neck, yet still I worry it, I pull out the threads, pluck and pull and release them to the wind, the wind that shall never again find the neck of my father, my handsome father, for he is shielded from it, as he is shielded from me, for he is below the earth and has been for years and cares not for the ways I remember him, or remember remembering him.

MARRIED LOVE, II

....

There will come a day—let it be many years from now—
when our kids realize no married couple ever needed to
retreat at high noon behind their locked bedroom door to
discuss taxes.

It's a kind of parlor game, a question someone asks at the after-party, perhaps, lounging on couches, shoes off, everyone half-inebriated and half-enamored and not ready for the long night to die. *What's your hidden talent?* This is no invitation to brag—*I got straight A's in college, I can benchpress 220.* Oh no no no, you win this game by trotting out a bizarre and useless skill.

Laura can stand on one leg forever. She moves to the center of the room and slides one heel up the other thigh, squares off in tree pose and balances until we pelt her with pillows. Thisbe can recite the entire back cover of *Flowers in the Attic.* Gaylord can pour a glass of wine back into the bottle without spilling, even with his eyes closed (how he became aware of that skill God only knows— I've never seen him walk away from a full glass). Tommy, who asked the question in the first place, can do achingly beautiful armpit farts. He rises to tuck his wrist under his arm, writhes and contorts, creates and christens—*Here's a burner, here's a wet one*—while everyone laughs and calls out requests. *I'm gonna pee myself,* Ann warbles.

Which brings us to me. I used to hate this game because I couldn't think of a hidden talent. But that's only because my hidden talent is very hidden. I've got the biggest bladder you've never seen.

It's not a matter of "holding it." At home I pee as much as anybody. But when I go out with friends, I simply forget to pee. And then later someone mentions, say, the wallpaper in a certain bathroom and I think, I didn't see it. Or the next bathroom, or the next. I'll count back until I realize it's been six hours since I peed.

One time I needed an ultrasound and the nurse told me not to urinate beforehand because a full bladder elevates the baby, better for viewing. I didn't pee that whole morning and when the nurse gessoed the wand and lowered it to my abdomen, she shouted for the doctor, "Get in here!" Not about the baby, the baby was fine. About me: "Lookit the size of her bladder!" I never saw the pixelated screen but I like to imagine my supremely visible baby rising and falling, buoyed on a bladder-shaped raft.

Because I can go so long between pees, when I do pee, I pee forever. Like I'll hear someone enter the next stall, hear her unzip, sit, pee, wipe, flush, zip, and exit, and the whole time, I'll have been peeing. Like if I'd started peeing when you'd started reading this, I'd still be peeing.

RETURNING FROM SPRING BREAK, JUNIOR YEAR AT NOTRE DAME

Swapped the rosary on my bedpost for Mardi Gras beads.

I didn't have a grandpa, so I studied my friend Lara's. He dozed before the TV in his wool cardigan. He walked without lifting his feet from the floor. Sometimes in the afternoon he shuffled to the hall closet, ducked inside for a moment, then shuffled back to the couch. Lara's eyes didn't swerve from *Mighty Mouse*, but I had to know what Gramps was doing in that closet, I had to. The next time he *shhhed* open the door, I snuck up behind him. He whirled around, wild-eyed, but when he saw it was me, only me, he smiled. He allowed me to witness him easing from a coat pocket a palm-sized white paper bag, McDonald's. He noiselessly uncrimped the top, spread its mouth with his thumb and index finger, reached in and pinched out a single fry. I understood that he was sneaking it. I understood that we must hide things from the mommies and the daddies. He held it out to me, a tiny sword, cold as if pulled from the heart of a stone.

ORANGE-SHAPED HOLE

....

Yesterday I remembered an event from twenty-five years ago, when I lived in London for a semester, in a flat in Bayswater with six other college girls. I don't know what resuscitated this memory; I've been reading a lot of Brits lately, so maybe it was Virginia Woolf or E. M. Forster. Or then again, maybe nobody. Maybe there's no trail of smelling salts I could trace to that flat in Bayswater.

Anyway, one day I got a postcard from my Canadian cousin, a grad student at Trinity, in Dublin. Brendan wrote that he'd be visiting friends in London, and he'd look me up. Turns out his friends also lived in Bayswater, just one street over, so he invited me to their dinner party.

I don't remember what we ate or drank or discussed, I remember only the long table filled with high-spirited bohemians—intellectuals, internationals, the great unwashed—and how I yearned to be one of them. And I remember the hostess, wild-haired, a bit fleshy, but enviable, enviable. At one point she reached into the fruit bowl, plucked an orange, tossed it once in her palm, and then reared her arm back like a pitcher and heaved the orange at her transom window. It smashed through the glass, leaving an orange-shaped hole, and bounced down the hall. Everyone laughed. No one got up to clean the glass.

Why, at nineteen, did that strike me as the height of glamour? And why—this is even harder to parse—why, remembering it now, does it still? Now that I'm old enough to know better, and spend a good part of my day cleaning up others' messes. Further, why would I have forgotten this, and for so long?

And now I've handed you the orange. I'm sorry, but now it's your orange, too. You've just read of a woman remembering an orange thrown through a window, without knowing why she remembers this. You will either remember reading this and know why you remember reading this, or you will remember reading this and not know why you remember reading this, or you will not remember reading this, possibly forever.

11. AND I'VE BEEN SEARCHING CEASELESSLY FOR YOU EVER SINCE, MON AMOUR

1. Once, many years ago, I sat on the beach, reading and drinking a beer.

2. It was a breezeless afternoon so I decided to cool off by the water.

3. I left my book—a fat novel, *The Brothers Karamazov*—on my folding chair. I snugged my bottle of New-castle Brown Ale deeper into its red coozie and screwed the coozie an inch or two into the sand.

4. It was pleasant by the water's edge. The running sandpipers, with their legs puncturing the silk of the receding surf, reminded me of the jackhammer nee-dle of my mother's sewing machine.

5. Strolling back maybe ten minutes later, I could easily pick out my blue chair—the beach wasn't crowded—but not the dark lump of book.

6. Even standing beside my chair, I could see I couldn't see it.

7. I toed around in the sand. Nothing.

8. When I picked up my coozie, it was light, although the bottle hadn't tipped.

9. Someone had ignored my towel, my chair, my beach bag with its sunblock and keys and wallet.

10. But stole my fat Russian novel and drank my ale.

....

The A/C won't work, so I call a repairman. His name, he tells me at the door, is Matthew. I lead him to the office we added on ten years ago—it has a separate system—and point out the little trapdoor in the ceiling. He's up there a long, long time, and when he finds me in the kitchen, he's slick with sweat. He says that the access to the heating and cooling is way too small. Very hard to get up there, very hard to navigate once you're up there. And Matthew is a small man, not much taller than me. Worse, says Matthew, when the unit blows and needs to be replaced, the ceiling will need to come down. He wipes an elbow across his dripping forehead, then digs out his phone. He shows me a photo of his tape measure stretched across the A/C, then stretched across the joists: the A/C is wider. Matthew tells me he emailed a video to his buddies.

It's not desirable, I know, for one's house to provide lunch break entertainment for so jaded a guild as the A/C repairmen of Mississippi.

Matthew says a door should be cut high on the wall for repairs, because, as is, it's near impossible to change a coil or fan unit. He says this door would be at the ass end of the unit, but that that's better than nothing. He says that if he gains a few (here he pats his wet shirt, stuck to his abs) he couldn't squeeze up there, even with a shoehorn and a crock full of bacon grease. Matthew: it's possible that at this point I have a slight crush on Matthew. Small, trim men can be so appealing. Also, authority makes me horny.

I'm willing to concede that, in addition to heating and cooling, there are numerous subjects of which I'm ignorant. Several years ago, on vacation with my former college roommates, the five of us sat around the way we do, drinking and catching up. The quiz show *Who Wants to Be a Millionaire* had just begun airing. One of my roommates, Laura, a biologist and high school teacher, had auditioned for the show, graduating through several levels, though ultimately she wasn't chosen. She told how part of her was relieved because she would have been embarrassed in front of her students if she got tripped up on a simple question.

"Yeah," said Beth, director of social work for a big prison and a master of TV trivia, "I'm relieved, too. I mean, what if you used 'Phone a Friend' and there I was, your entertainment lifeline, and I couldn't come up with, like, the name of the car on *Knight Rider*?"

Denise, former captain of the Notre Dame soccer team and now CMO of a Fortune 500 company, said, "Right, as your sports lifeline, how bad would it have sucked if I didn't know who won the World Cup?"

They kept talking about Laura's audition as I worked

it out: "You mean—you mean I'm the only one who's not a . . . what do you call it . . ." (I'd never seen the show) "lifeline?"

The girls exchanged looks: Uh oh.

Laura laid a palm, chilled from her gin and tonic, on my knee. "Oh, B.A., honey. Don't take it personally. After all, come on"—she smiled, not unkindly—"what are your lifeline areas?"

Let's see. There's poetry. Metrical *and* free verse. So there. And babies. I'm good at babies, at making them and birthing them. I used to be good at making milk for them, too. I recall how my babies would fall asleep while nursing, how their lips would loosen from my nipple, how I could see into the sweet pink grottoes of their mouths, their tongues still flexing a time or two, the pearly milk pooling there or sometimes running from the corner of their lips. *Eat all you want: I'll make more.* And let's not forget I am very good at cookies. My friend Lee Durkee says I bake the best snickerdoodles he's ever tasted. And he's never even tried my lemon poppyseed. Or, sweet Jesus, my gingersnaps.

My areas of expertise are scrolling through my mind as Matthew scrolls through photos on his phone, detailing the problems. I'm nodding. Which is to say, faking, which I do when flummoxed by technology or mechanics. I'm like a dog—a bitch, in fact, for I feel ungainly and femaley—a bitch, reading her master, trying to glean her fate from everything but words. If Master points to Car, does this mean Park, or Pound? Matthew says Freon and BTUs and then several unrecognizable terms. I'm still nodding when he leaves.

So I track down the original contractor. I'm hoping he camouflaged some magic attic access, stairs that descend when you pull the sconce beside the bookcase, which probably revolves.

He did not. He built this addition ten years ago and can't remember why we settled on this design. Neither can I. That's another thing I'm not good at: remembering. He thinks we knew access would be hard but decided it was worth it for roofline aesthetics. Hmm, I think. I do like aesthetics. I nod. He thinks we decided that the unit would last maybe twenty years or more, and that we'd deal with replacing it then, cutting a hole through the sheetrock. No biggie. I nod, thinking, Would I really have agreed to sew a dress knowing the zipper wasn't long enough? Would I really have thought, Hey, we'll just cut the dress off when I'm done? But the longer he talks, the more familiar the idea sounds. I say, Do we need to build that access door Matthew suggested? The contractor huffs a laugh. No, he says, most certainly not. I nod. This contractor—I notice for the first time—this contractor is a handsome man. A big man, tall, with a generous belly pressing taut his striped polo. I bet he shops at stores called Big and Tall. Big and Tall and Yummy. I would like to help him choose his striped polos. *Try this one on. And this.*

If there was a planet where all the repairmen were repairwomen, I'd rocket there, never to return. I'd still be puzzled when something broke and they explained—I'm nobody's lifeline, after all—but I wouldn't be additionally puzzled by my failures as a feminist.

So we're good then? the contractor asks.

I nod. I'm a good dog. I offer him a cookie.

"IF YOU WERE BORN CATHOLIC, YOU'LL ALWAYS BE CATHOLIC"

My husband sits up after changing the van's busted tire, grease on his forehead and I think—though it's been twenty years—Ash Wednesday.

DISHARMONY

My mother and I argued about her eHarmony profile. I thought she should list her age as seventy-four, not because she couldn't pull off sixty-four—she could, she's a beautiful woman—but because if she did meet someone, she'd be beginning their relationship with a lie.

But I don't *feel* seventy-four, she'd insist.

Our argument was not long-lived. The lumps turned out to be cancer. After her double mastectomy, she underwent a slow rotation before the full-length mirror. After that, she deleted her profile.

The biker bar on Airport Boulevard in West Mobile always attracted a rough crowd, but that crowd seemed particularly rough. Still, I stacked my quarters on a pool table in the dim, cool back room.

By the time I'd gotten my beer, my turn was up. I walked over to the guy running the table. A brown vinyl case leaned in the corner. He'd brought his own cue.

"Pete," he said, and we shook. He was big and grizzled, black T-shirted belly looping over his belt, red-brown beard and mustache, but he looked out from a pair of youngish eyes, maybe mid-twenties, like me. I thumbed my quarters into the tray, shoved it in with the heel of my hand, and we listened to the balls clatter from the table's belly into its mouth.

"Lag for break?" I asked.

"No," he said. "You go."

I reached in to pull out the molars as he laid the rack on the felt.

Someone walked by and touched his shoulder.

"Crowded tonight," I said.

"Yeah." He snugged the fifteen in the triangle. "They're having a wake."

"A wake? Wow."

"Yeah. Guy wrecked. On his bike. Just down the street."

I selected a cue and chalked it, noticing on a nearby table a framed photo: a big man in a sleeveless leather vest, straddling a motorcycle, cigarette skewering his grin.

He noticed me noticing. "Yeah. That's him."

"Wow," I said again.

He lifted the triangle, flipped it once, and popped it into its slot.

"Friend of yours?" I bent over the table.

"Not really."

I drew my cue back, did three quick elbow-saws to warm up.

"He was my old man."

I'd have lost anyway—did I mention he'd brought his own cue?—but now I had an excuse. Imagine telling someone that right before they break.

WHAT I THINK ABOUT WHEN SOMEONE USES "PUSSY" AS A SYNONYM FOR "WEAK"

At the deepest part of the deepest part, I rocked shut like a stone. I'd climbed as far inside me as I could. Everything else had fallen away. Midwife, husband, bedroom, world: quaint concepts. My eyes were clamshells. My ears were clapped shut by the palms of the dead. My throat was stoppered with bees. I was the fox caught in the trap, and I was the trap. Chewing off a leg would have been easier than what I now required of myself. I understood I was alone in it. I understood I would come back from there with the baby, or I wouldn't come back at all. I was beyond the ministrations of loved ones. I was beyond the grasp of men. Even their prayers couldn't penetrate me. The pain was such that I made peace with that. I did not fear death. Fear was an emotion, and pain had scalded away all emotion. I chose. In order to come back with the baby, I had to tear it out at the root. Understand, I did this without the aid of my hands.

LOW-BUDGET CAR DEALERSHIP COMMERCIAL

My high school theater troupe was offered the gig, fifty dollars each to play volleyball on the beach by Lake Michigan, with a giant pickup truck in the background.

It's shameful but I've always loved an audience. With the camera rolling I entered a never-before-and-never-again zone of skill and sass. At one point the camera guy ran to my side, whipping his black power cord behind him like a snake, and shot a close-up of my supplicant wrists perfectly bumping a ball to the center.

Months later I saw the commercial. After the shot of my wrists, the camera cut to the triumphant, lightly misted face of a model with absolutely zero teenage acne.

1. Snow churned and swirled, that December day in 1967, when the two-engine plane containing Otis Redding and his band, the Bar-Kays, took off from Cleveland. Just a few miles short of the Madison, Wisconsin airport, the plane crashed into Lake Monona. Three days prior, he'd recorded "Dock of the Bay." It would become history's first number one posthumous hit.

2. Otis was twenty-six, two years younger than I was when I lived in Madison on a poetry fellowship. Sometimes I'd run around the lake and fret. Twenty-eight already! Where was my "Dock of the Bay"?

3. I was running around Monona (thirteen miles) and later Lake Mendota (seventeen miles) because I was marathon training. Now I'm glad that I didn't merely jog on a treadmill or endlessly loop a track, because one summer, years later, I returned, stood on the goose-shit-slick grass and took it all in, the bandages of fog snagged on the cattails, the buoys, the crew team unzipping the water, the Lego-sized houses on the far shore, and thought: I *ran* around this motherfucker. With my *legs*.

4. I was lucky to have the fellowship, but each day felt dogged by anxiety. What was to become of me? I'd walk to the university to teach, down State Street, past the Capitol. Sometimes, to warm up, I'd loiter in the Lands' End outlet, which sold catalog returns. Even discounted, the robes were more than I could pay. I pawed through the rack of even cheaper robes which bore botched monograms—would I rather sip my coffee as CLN or PL or MMB?—when there it was, my Christmas miracle, BAF, I shit you not.

5. When Otis recorded "Dock of the Bay," he and his cowriter, Steve Cropper, hadn't finished the last verse, so Otis whistled, ad-lib. They planned to get back into the studio after the concert in Madison. You can almost see them at Stax, shutting down the four-track, the console, killing the lights, *We'll finish 'er up on Monday.* Later, when Cropper, mourning, produced the song, he kept the whistling. Now it's the most famous whistled passage in any song.

6. Each day my fellowship was a day shorter, and I still had no "Dock of the Bay." I'd applied to somewhere between sixteen and seventeen thousand bazillion teaching jobs. I, who hated the cold, had further materials requested from a school called Bemidji State.

According to the website, the northern Minnesota town, right below Canada, was nicknamed Brrr-midji.

7. What the marathon permitted was exquisitely calibrated pain.

8. The robe wasn't the only lucky thing. There was also the desk. In my cheap apartment, I'd rigged two milk crates to write on. Now, running around Mendota, I found a desk that someone had dragged to the curb. But there was nothing wrong with it: large, solid, a beautiful blond wood, with "Folsom Brothers, 1947" branded beneath. Back in my apartment, it pressed the floor away from my face with four strong legs. Some days it felt like the only substantial thing in my life.

9. On lake runs, I wore Band-Aids on my frigid nipples or they'd bleed from chafing. But other blood stopped altogether no period for months. Also, my big toenails popped off. I painted ovals of polish where my nails should've been.

10. The crash also killed Otis's pilot, his manager, and four out of five Bar-Kays. Plenty of others have drowned in that cold cold lake. Quite a few ice fish-

ermen, for instance. The one yelling over his shoulder for his friends to stay back, testing the paunchy ice with an insulated boot. The one still gripping the handles of his snowmobile. Twin brothers in the red pickup, serenaded by the Eagles all the way to the bottom. Maurice Field, University of Wisconsin class of '21. His Model T, furry with algae but in photos appearing perfectly drivable, rests only thirty feet down. The 1928 alumni newsletter states that Field drowned "trying to save a young girl in the backseat." States that Field's body was recovered and buried in Sun Prairie, Wisconsin.

11. I wanted to keep it forever, the desk, but at the year's end, I had to give it up. I dragged it to the curb and labeled it, "Free to good home." I walked slowly back inside and felt a pang—so many hours writing in my robe at that desk!—and lifted the curtain to say good-bye. It was already gone.

12. The newsletter didn't mention what became of the girl.

13. The only band member to survive the crash was the trumpeter. He was the one who played taps.

My mother seined the waters of our childhoods. She gathered everything into the nets of her fingers: schoolwork, artwork, mementos. My mother did not recycle. Nor did she dispose. She was indisposed to it. Gathered now, it seems a kind of evidence, but of what? Consider the card she saved from the nurse who helped deliver me: *Second daughter! Looks like you'll have to wait for next time to get that son!* Consider my mother pasting that into my baby book. It would seem to imply I've been a disappointment since the moment I was born.

THE NEIGHBOR, THE CHICKENS, AND THE FLAMES

This tale begins with the chickens. Last April, my neighbor Lauren mail-ordered them, in the form of baby chicks. Those cool spring nights, she corralled them in her bathtub. When they grew, she moved them to her fenced-in backyard, to roam by day and, by night, to cozy up in the coop she'd built off the back of her house.

These weren't typical barnyard cluckers. Lauren had six exotic breeds, all hens: a brown pair with puffs of feathers at their ankles, like Clydesdales; a black pair with overlapping, iridescent, fish-scale feathers; a white pair, elongated like they'd been crossed with seagulls; etc. They were as impressive as Lauren herself. She's British, her regal accent cutting through our Mississippi drawls. She's a river erosion scientist, and when she isn't saving our rivers, she's transforming her modest backyard (the same dimensions as ours) into an Eden with white icicle radishes, red samurai carrots, beanstalks Jack would envy. Also, she powerlifts. When you look at her, you think "specimen" or "anatomical model." You think rheumatology students with clipboards should trail her, muttering *trapezius* and *rectus femoris* as she lumberjacks around in sports bra and running shorts.

Lauren's children, too, are lean, strong, and sun-

brown. They garden beside her all weekend. My children
—soft, pale, unathletic nongardeners—play with Lauren's
children for short intervals, before needing a rest. My children are fond of Lauren, but, quick learners, they say, "No,
thanks, I'm not hungry" when offered a popsicle. Like my
store-bought popsicles, hers are red and green. Unlike my
popsicles, her reds and greens derive from beets and kale.
My children are also wise to Lauren's Easter Bunny. Last
year, at her party, when the kids began shucking open
the plastic eggs, they found either cut up strawberries or
Frosted Mini-Wheats. Out of earshot of the children, she
told me that she'd have preferred *unfrosted* Mini-Wheats,
but, well, blimey, it was Easter, after all.

So that's Lauren. And those are her chickens, dining
on heirloom-radish-top-compost, powerlaying matching
pairs of pastel eggs.

Yet they preferred us. Mornings, almost as soon as
she'd bicycled off to work, her chickens would fly—though
fly hardly conveys their fluttery, cumbersome heave—to
the top of the chain-link. After perching, they'd swoop
down to peck through our unmown grass for bugs. They'd
chill with us most of the day, but by the time Lauren biked
home, they'd be back in their coop. As if they, too, were a
little scared of Lauren.

One hen seemed particularly fond of our company.
She had rust-colored feathers, quite long, ornamental-

seeming. I liked to watch her quick-stepping in her feathery bolero, occasionally pausing as if to model for a weathervane. Once she flew to the platform of my kids' swing set and peered at the slide. Instantly I knew I'd pay a goodly sum to watch her tuck her legs and careen down. I swear to God, she considered it. But my kids spooked her by running over.

She seemed to be preparing for defection. Working at my desk one morning, I heard loud clucking. Glad for the distraction, I went outside and found, snug against our house, a bald patch where she'd breasted some woodchips away and left, like a calling card, a feather.

The next day, I was sorta working when her clucking got louder, then louder yet. She was summoning me. When I got outside, she was waddling away, and in her roost lay a large sand-colored egg. I picked it up, palming its warmth.

I intended to return it to Lauren's coop, I'm certain. Yet somehow, I found myself carrying it to our kitchen, where I washed it, fried it, and fed it to my family while they watched cartoons. You wouldn't think one-fifth of an egg would satisfy, but you've never tasted an egg curated by Lauren. The yolk was the hue of a marigold.

That hen became our pet. The kids fed her Cheetos. We even competed to name her. Beyoncé is not what I'd have chosen, but we'd agreed before setting out Monopoly that the winner got naming rights, and Thomas had a hotel on Park Place.

Each day, for three days, Beyoncé—like a hen from a fairy tale—laid me a golden egg. Each day, for three days, I—like the lazy commoner, the covetous neighbor—snuck it, fried it, then spooned it into the mouths of my loved ones. Did I realize I was stealing? Yes, of course, I realized I was stealing. Lauren had earned these eggs; she'd nursed balls of fluff, she'd bought their feed, she'd built the coop—the Taj Majal of coops—with her own tools and triceps, fortifying it to keep out raccoons and whatnot. She never guessed her neighbor was the proverbial fox in the henhouse.

Then she did guess. We share a babysitter, so maybe the sitter ratted me out after seeing me with, well, egg on my face. Probably Lauren was already suspicious, each afternoon counting eggs in clipped consonants, nestling them in the Noah's Ark of recycled cardboard, two by two, by two, by . . . one. Anyway, she never confronted me. She simply took matters into her own hands. She clipped the hens' wings. She wouldn't want them flying into the street, she said, and getting flattened by a car.

What happened was way worse than a car. Last January, coldest night of the year, long after I'd gone to bed, I woke to my husband slamming open our bedroom door, yelling, "The neighbor's house is on fire!" He grabbed his phone, began mashing buttons. "I'm calling 911!" I jumped up and ran outside. Over Lauren's house, the night sky slashed with roaring orange, flames taller than her chimney. Yet her house was dark with sleep. I pounded and kicked at her door, and when she yanked it open, I yelled about the fire. She whirled and sprinted out the back. So I went in and pulled her sleeping children from their beds. They were frightened, and began crying, but I carried them to the front yard, all of us in our pajamas, and hugged them to comfort and to warm.

Soon, more neighbors, and the siren, and the firefighters jumping down as the truck pulled to the hydrant. I left Lauren's kids with my husband and ran around back, found her hosing down her house, her face glazed with tears which flickered orange in the flames. She'd kept the blaze from spreading. Now she let the firemen take over. We stood and watched them work.

"I'm so stupid," she said, after several minutes. "I didn't want the chickens to freeze. I gave them a heat lamp. It must have caught the newspapers on fire." She surveyed the coop's cinders, her brick wall singed and smoking. "In another few seconds, our roof would have caught fire. The whole house would have gone up."

You might be thinking that it's a pretty big coincidence that Lauren robs us of Beyoncé and then her chickens get flame-broiled. But it wasn't like that. The two hens that

escaped the blaze died from smoke. The whole neighbor-
hood felt subdued, smelled charred. And the fire haunted
me. For weeks, my nightmares crackled red with flames,
flames, flames.

The day after the fire, Lauren came by. She wanted to
thank us, she said, for saving their lives. She gave us a gift
card to the sweet shop. I'm guessing it was her first time
there ("What is this thing called 'ice cream,' Mommy?").
She'd already ordered more chicks, though they wouldn't
ship until April.

Grown now, they're great producers, at least that's
what she says. But I wouldn't know. I don't even meet
their eyes when they stand at the fence and cluck. I've
been burned once. I know how that fairy tale ends.

MARRIED LOVE, III

....

As we lower onto the December-cold pleather seats of the minivan, we knock hands: both of us reaching to turn on the other's seat warmer first.

—*I can't find my wine glass. My favorite wine glass.*

—The one with the glass beads glued on?

—*That's the one. I think the maid took it.*

—The maid didn't take it.

—*Yes, she did. The Polish maid. She took it.*

—The maid didn't take the wine glass, Mom. If she was going to steal, she'd steal something valuable. Jewelry or money. But she's not stealing. And she certainly didn't take your wine glass. You've misplaced it. It'll turn up.

⊚⊘

—*I found my wine glass.*

—Yeah? Where?

—*In the cabinet. She put it back.*

ANOTHER REASON I LOVE MY MOTHER

At the baby shower, she rejects the pink M&Ms, because pink M&Ms are "unnatural."

She was an antique carpet merchant: another occupation I'd never considered. Maybe sixty, she wore a sleek silver bob and an embroidered cloak. We'd begun chatting as we tried to hail taxis. Christ, where were they? Icy wind zephyred off Lake Michigan and fingered between the buttons of my thin coat, wrung my neck like a muffler.

"There are some very pretty mid-range carpets," she said, in response to something I'd said, eyes on Columbus for a streak of yellow.

The street cleared for a moment, the cars across the intersection drawn short at the light, impatient horses at the gate.

"Mid-range?" I asked.

"Fifteen to thirty."

I'd gone to the museum benefit with my friend because a guy we knew from catering could sneak us through the loading dock. Free drinks galore, she'd promised he'd promised. My red dress was a tight little number, but I was young enough that it didn't look cheap. Wavering candlelight, unwavering regard of husbands over their wives' shoulders as I'd slow-danced with my friend, my beautiful Latina friend. In the middle of the party she'd gone to the bathroom and hadn't reappeared. I waited, watched a caterer skirt the dance floor, stumble on a chair leg. I knew they'd probably done whippets off the whipped cream canisters.

Finally she turned up, giggling, trailing a man in a tux. She wanted to leave with him, I could tell, but felt bad that I'd have to take the el alone in my tipsy high heels. When he handed me a twenty for a cab, she practically sprinted to the coat check.

Now I just wanted to be home. The taxi line at the museum had been so long I thought I'd have better luck around the block. The carpet merchant, I assumed, had assumed the same.

A taxi appeared and I stepped forward, raising my palm, but it was occupied so I dodged the arc of slush. The carpet merchant hadn't moved. She must have checked the "for hire" light. I always forgot to do that.

Another pause in traffic. By Christ, it was cold. I'd lost my gloves so I shrugged my hands up in my sleeves. I probably looked like an amputee. Also, my borrowed stilettos hurt like a mother. Another full taxi streaked by, another, and then traffic cleared again. I crossed my arms, buried my fists in my armpits. "Tell me something about carpets."

She lifted a shoulder. "The best way to clean a fine

carpet. Is simple, really. You carry it outside, and lay it top side down, on a fresh fallen snow." I looked at her, hoping she wasn't putting me on. For the first time I caught the spice of an accent, Eastern European maybe. "You leave it there for a day and a night and a day, and when you peel it back, the carpet is clean, clean, and the snow beneath dark as coal.'

I could picture it all, a clearing between the snow-fretted pines, the servants squatting to tuck the knotted fringe, then crimping the edge, rolling it in, scrolling and scrolling, hand over hand, feet crunching through the shadow the carpet had shed. How they stand and count to three before heaving the felled tree to their shoulders, staggering briefly, then trudging back to the villa where, from an upper window, the countess observes.

Across the intersection a taxi winked. The carpet merchant had summoned it with a gloved finger. She turned to me and gestured to the approaching taxi, but we'd arrived at the same time, so I shook my head.

She opened the door, then turned back. "Headed north?"

I shook my head again.

"Right," she said. "Farewell."

I watched her bend into the cab, lean forward to say something to the driver and then lean back, resting her head on the seat. I kept watching as the taxi sleighed away, down Columbus, against the backdrop of Lake Michigan frozen and flat, endless, really, an endless carpet of fresh fallen snow.

Already I was learning that some of the things I was learning weren't things I'd need to know.

HOME BUTTON

When we snuggle, my left hand finds purchase on his back cyst.

SOME CHILDHOOD DREAMS
REALLY DO COME TRUE

....

THEN

I wanted to be a mermaid. But first, I needed the tits and the hair. Hair long enough that it rivered in naked curves down my naked chest while I lounged on a rock, luring sailors with my song.

NOW

I have tits, and hair down to my ass.

You're probably expecting me to end with something depressing like, "Yet I never lounge on rocks, luring sailors with my song. In fact, I never even sing in the shower."

But you'd be wrong. Dead wrong. I *must* have become a mermaid: look at my wrinkly skin. What could have caused me to wrinkle, if not hours spent submerged, frolicking in the sea?

It was his wife's birthday and seven of us were having dinner, seated around a festive table. Our friend the memoirist felt moved to make a toast.

"I'd like to make a toast," he began, lifting his glass. "I'd like to tell a story about our first date, which took place on my wife's birthday, thirteen years ago tonight."

"Aww," said one of us, probably more than one of us. We'd drunk some wine. It was the right time of the evening for sweet reminiscing. And our friend was a memoirist, a professional reminiscer. This was going to be good.

Encouraged, he continued, "Thirteen years ago, I took my beautiful wife to a Mexican restaurant."

We all turned—she'd been placed at the other end of the table—anticipating her smile. She has a sweet smile. And in fact she was smiling, but not the way we'd anticipated.

"Well," she said, softly. Softly, but precisely. "The Mexican restaurant was one of our early dates, for sure."

This gave him pause. "That was our first date."

"Um," she said, "no . . . but that was *one* of our first dates."

"The Mexican restaurant. On your birthday. Our first date."

"No," she said, "not exactly."

"The Mexican restaurant wasn't our first date?"

She shook her head, still smiling. She's a good bit younger than the memoirist, with long dark hair and the sweetest smile I know. But you shouldn't underestimate her. And it might be worth mentioning her first novel will be published in April.

"If that wasn't our first date, what was?"

A pause. "Remember the bad sushi?"

We watched him remember. It was almost painful.

He lowered his glass of wine to the table and sat back in his chair. He said, "Well, I guess I'm not going to make my toast now. I guess I'm not going to tell my story. And I had it all planned out and everything."

"Oh, come on," we said. "You can still say what you were going to say."

"No," he said.

"Oh, come on. Please."

"No, I can't. Not anymore, I can't. Which is too bad, you know. It was going to be a really good toast."

I remember being in the car on the way to my sister's surprise funeral In the backseat, I think. I can't imagine who was driving. At a stop sign my head swiveled to a flicker in the roadside greenery: a fox, poking its snout from between two bushes. I thought, or chose to think. That is my sister. That is my sister, come back in animal form to tell me it's okay. She's okay. I'll be okay.

But it was not okay. She was not okay. I would not be okay. I would not be okay for so long that when okay arrived it couldn't place me. It looked right past the veil of shivering leaves, my long red snout, my gloved paws swiping tears into my little black mouth.

DAUGHTER, THEY'LL USE EVEN YOUR OWN GAZE TO WOUND YOU

....

1. Chicago, IL

My high school teacher loved that I loved libraries, so she promised she'd bring me to her alma mater's. One Saturday, we took the train in and she donned white gloves to turn manuscript pages while I roamed the stacks, inhaling that dear dusty library funk. Wait: did I hear footsteps? When I was sure I'd been mistaken, I pulled out a heavy tome. There, thrusting through, a tube of flesh. Years later a librarian would tell me paraphilic activity is quite common in her place of work. Just in case you're wondering if I was special.

2. South Bend, IN

My college roomies and I were three beers in, walking from campus to Brigit's, a bar so seedy that, after graduation, it'd be condemned. A Tercel pulled over and the interior light flicked on to halo a man consulting a map. Good Catholics, we inquired if he needed directions. *Can you show me where I am on my map?* So we stepped closer and discovered where he was on his map: through the center, dickly. I'm guessing it was Denise who began laughing, or maybe Beth, but in seconds we were all hooting, we could barely stumble away, shrieking and pounding one another. He screeched through the intersection, the light still red.

3. Fayetteville, AR

From dawn till noon I'd reviewed Wordsworth, cramming for my comp exam, and now as I ran through the park, sonnets metered out my pounding feet. A bicycle came from behind, a man swiveling to see my face. At the top of the hill, he stopped, turned, and coasted back toward me. I could see his fist gripping something low on his belly. What zinged through my head: a bouquet. But that was no bouquet. I didn't even slow as he passed, just averted my eyes.

I'd run nine miles that day with one to go.
I guess I'd learned by then what women know.

MARRIED LOVE, IV

....

Morning: bought a bag of frozen peas to numb my husband's sore testicles after his vasectomy.

Evening: added thawed peas to our carbonara.

At twelve, I learned my father had had a brother who died of cirrhosis. In all those years, my father hadn't spoken of him. I knew I had an aunt and cousins in New Jersey, but somehow I wasn't concerned with who their father was. He just wasn't, that's all. Fathers were different when I was growing up. They worked all day, they came home late. You'd been fed, you'd bathed and put on your nightgown. *Give your father a goodnight kiss, Beth Ann.*

My father's father was a dental surgeon, served overseas for four years during World War II. Once I asked my father what that was like.

"We managed," he said.

"But what was it like," I pressed, "having your father gone for so much of your childhood?"

He shrugged. "We got used to it."

"But what was a day like? What did you do for fun?"

"We played Japs."

"Jacks? You played jacks?"

"Japs. We played Japs. My friends in the building and I, we ran around, ducking into doors, crouching with invisible guns. Rat-a-tat-tat-tat-tat. We killed Japs all day."

What was it like having your father miss your childhood? Funny I had to ask.

I KNEW A WOMAN

Everything she had was better than everything the rest of us had. Not by a lot. But by enough.

When I was a girl with a book in my hand I could go to a place so deep no one could follow. No one cared to, except my mother, an affectionate woman who smarted at her lack of companionship. She must have fretted to watch me wading out, leaving her behind. She must have stood on the shore and wrung her hands, the waves retreating, the sand beneath her feet eroding grain by grain by grain. She must have felt bereft to see her own dear daughter sinking, even the long dark locks, eel-graceful.

Sometimes, in the deep, I'd hear an echo for a long time before I recognized what I'd been hearing: my name. My mother, calling my human name.

Yes, Mom? I'd lift the globes of my eyes.

It's time to set the table, Honey.

Okay.

I'd place the book belly-down and rise, though I could see (we both could see) dinner was still a good way off.

He was dying, he would soon be dead. My mother had told me so. She had prepared me to expect the urine-colored eyes, the distended belly, the dementia and palsied hands. I pulled up a chair to his hospital deathbed. I wondered if I should say "I love you." That phrase corresponded to nothing, but I didn't want guilt later. I didn't want to suffer because the last time I saw my father, I didn't tell him I loved him. I could hear my future voice, *If only I'd told him I loved him.* I wanted to spare my future me, whom I did love. So I told him I loved him and I left.

Sometimes, in grad school, we'd sit around talking about who was publishing what where. This always ended bitterly. Bitter feelings all around. Once, a rival poet (we were all suddenly rivals) confessed he had a secret font. He called it the "Publish Me" font. He claimed that every time he submitted poems in this font, they got accepted. Of course we asked him the name of this font, but he smugly declined to share.

EXPIRATION DATE

Every time my mother visits now, she brings a stack of yellowed papers. My girlhood artwork, some of it forty years old. We flip through together: the Mother's Day menu I cooked her when I was ten. A letter from camp. A coupon book, crayoned for her birthday, 1979—free foot massage, free breakfast in bed. I'd given the coupons the expiration date of New Year's Eve, 1999, the most impossible distance conceivable, a day I knew would never come to pass.

We don't talk about why she's going through her attic. Her prognosis is good. But she's seventy-five.

Last summer, at the consultation before my mother's double mastectomy, I questioned the surgeon about the silicone implants. They don't last forever, right? How long before Mom needs a replacement? *Fifteen years,* he said, meeting my eyes. No further questions.

New Year's Eve, 1999: not the impossibility it had seemed. That date has been ceded to the territory of the past. The same will hold true, eventually, for the day my mother will expire.

I'll be alone, curator of the archives. Bearer of this coupon good for a free hug.

The week of my twenty-third birthday, I met up with Elaine and Kathleen in Barcelona, where Elaine was teaching conversational English. One night, her language school hosted a party on the roof. We arrived early to help, and I was given garlic to peel for mayonnaise. That's the first reason that night is memorable: I'd eaten my share of mayonnaise but never made it. In fact, I'm not sure I knew it *could* be made. Now, next to me, a good-looking Spaniard was whisking lemon juice into yolks, the hair on his strong brown wrist glistening in the lowering sun. We were translating the recipe so I could make it back home. Behind us someone was strumming a guitar, tightening a string, strumming again, this as the Spaniard streamed olive oil with one hand, whisking with the other, "And then you—I'm not sure how to say in English, you mix these two that should no be mixed, you need very fast, *emulsionar,*" and my "Oh, it's the same, the same in English, emulsify."

After my lesson, I refilled my sangria, then drifted to the parapet where Kathleen and Elaine leaned, marveling at the zany evening traffic, daredevil motorcyclists—some of them couriers or food deliverers—squeezing between speeding cars. I said, "I feel like I'm waiting for an accident to happen."

Only seconds later we heard the shriek of abrupt tires followed by a thud, and we turned to see a body scudding across an intersection. A man, on his back, as if shot from a cannon. I'm sure we screamed. The rest of the party rushed over, but traffic blocked our view. We could see only a motorcycle on its side. Soon an ambulance arrived—its siren unexpectedly on a different key, a siren with a Catalonian accent. After a few minutes, the ambulance squealed away. Somberly, everyone on the roof ghosted back to the party. When the guitarist started singing, all his songs were sad songs.

The next afternoon, at the language school, we learned the motorcyclist had died. I was surprised, though all day I'd been chased by that thud, what I now knew to be a body embracing a speeding car. It was the first time I'd heard death. Which is another reason I remember that night.

The third is this. That was one of the last times I'd see Elaine. We'd been such good friends the year prior, when the three of us taught English in the Czech Republic, and met up on weekends to booze and laugh and kiss bartenders. I knew we'd be friends forever. But soon thereafter, Elaine got a serious boyfriend, twenty years older. She seemed to age, overnight, on the inside. She didn't want to stalk around with us anymore, stiletto heels punching holes in the map of Europe. Or her boyfriend didn't want her to, same difference. I think he thought she shouldn't mix with me, that I was a bad influence. Which I was. In those days, I could cause an accident merely by waiting for it to happen.

WHEN PEOPLE BEMOAN THE
COMMODIFICATION OF ART

....

I think of picnicking at Blair's studio. Reaching for my second slice of watermelon, I saw some lines—a black Sharpie?—crossing the green rind.

"Did you *draw* on this, Blair?" I asked.

"Oh, sure," she said, with a shrug. "Melon skin is one of my favorite mediums."

When our daughter was nine, she contracted a brain-eating amoeba after swimming in a neighbor's pond. Or so she believed. There was no talking her out of it, though Lord knows I tried. The next day, she wouldn't join the kids leaping through the sprinkler. *Go have fun*, I told her. She shook her head. She was done with fun. I found it, at that point, almost cute.

It grew less cute, acutely, over the following days. Fretting, I conceived the cure: a water park. Who could watch kids shriek down the slide and not join them? She could. She read Greek myths, hunkered under a towel to ward off splashes, deaf to our pleas. She led the way to the car, her thighs bearing welts from the chaise's plastic straps.

When I discovered she was faking her bath—she'd lock the door, run the water, then emerge, dressed and dry—I became truly concerned. She gave up nothing when questioned, as if explaining would jeopardize our lives, too. I showed her articles detailing symptoms she didn't have. She shook us off. *Maybe she just wants attention*, said my mother. Maybe . . . but it didn't feel that way. Her light was on at odd hours; she was having problems sleeping. While she was too young to develop serious b.o., her bangs clumped greasily, and the back of her hair was pasty with white gunk. I felt embarrassed, and ashamed at feeling embarrassed. Should we consult a child therapist? One day, in the bathroom, trying to get through to her while trying to get a comb through her hair, I grabbed the fist-sized tangle and shook. *I'm going to have to cut this off,* I snarled. *Do you understand? Unless you get over this silly fear.* I wanted to rattle her head until the crazy fell out. To lock the door, turn on the faucet, and force her under: to prove she wouldn't die.

Clearly, I needed a break, so my husband and I met our friends at the bar. Many of them don't have children and they like when we complain about ours. But our friends didn't laugh. Instead, they recalled their own childhood brushes with rare infectious diseases. Our friends, smart and successful adults who began life as smart and weird children, felt for our daughter, our smart and weird daughter, dedicated to her dying.

One friend, drunkish, a successful sports writer, said, *Give me your phone. I can handle this.*

How, we asked. *How can you handle this?*

He said, *I'm going to tell her*—here he deepened his already deep voice, right in front of us his face sobered, sovereigned—*This is Dr. Thompson, Anna Claire. There is no such disease as a brain-eating amoeba. Now, I command you to put aside these childish fears, and rise, and shampoo your hair until it squeaks.*

Mesmerized, I passed him my phone. He put it on speaker and we all leaned in. We could hear the ringing It rang and rang and rang.

She must be in the shower, I said for a laugh.

Laughter wasn't the best medicine, but it would be all I'd have her after. In time, she'd get over her fear, on her own. By then, the sickness had spread, because something was eating my brain, too: knowing that she'd had her first problem I couldn't solve, and knowing there would only be more of them, and knowing that she'd known that already, and had decided, in her mercy, to spare me.

PASS THE VODKA

Inside Wendy's freezer: a bottle of vodka and a dead cat in plastic wrap. The cat she froze so she can bury it when she returns to Florida, where the cat was happy, before Wendy divorced and moved away to make a fresh start.

Five weeks after her sister died, she was scheduled to speak at a writers' conference. She'd been invited nearly a year before. Her husband kept assuring her she could cancel: she was grieving. Too true.

But she was getting better, sort of. By this point, she only started crying when someone approached and told her how sorry they were to hear about her sister. Unfortunately, she lived in a small town, so this happened every time she went anywhere, even to the stupid grocery store, that's her in the freezer section, door wrenched open, doubled over in the mist, tears pocking the stupid faces of the stupid frozen pizzas, all because another stupid couple had come and put their warm and stupid arms around her.

She kept not being able to write the email, the email to the conference director, the one that began "sorry" and "sister" and "sudden." She kept not being able to write it until finally it was too late, she had to board that plane.

When she disembarked, a college student waited, holding a sign with her name. He grinned, recognizing her from her author photo, and lifted her duffel from her shoulder, then drove her in his doorless Jeep over an arcing bridge to the island, the pretty little island. As he sped along, he questioned her, but only about her books. Her books! Her news had not reached this outlying kingdom. She answered, listened to her answers. Her advice was sound. Her voice unwavering. Her body angled toward his. She was impersonating a woman whose sister was extant, and workshopping her impersonation.

She passed. She taught a class on metaphor which was well received. She dined with the other writers and when they laughed she laughed and observed herself laughing and thought, *This is . . . mirthful*. She drank wine at the wine-drinking times and signed books at the book-signing times. Beach walks occurred. Occasionally she felt something hysterical winging up through her throat, the propulsion of it could almost lift her off the ground, a howl, or a laugh, or some combination new to the human register, but she did not vocalize those vowels.

After three days, she returned home. The plane bounced twice as it landed. She gathered her belongings from the overhead bin. To prepare to meet the faces she would meet, she stepped into her suit of grief. She pulled it up, over her legs, her hips. She threaded her arms into the sleeves of grief. She huffed it over her back. She snugged it around her shoulders. She buttoned herself tight. Its weight was dear. Dear, dear, dear. She would wear it forever now.

WHEN THEY GROW UP

My oldest child will hate me because I wrote an entire book about her. My middle child will hate me because I wrote hardly a word about him. But the baby; ah, the baby. When I write about him, I call it fiction, and I'm always sure to mention he has a big penis.

—He placed his beer on the pool's lip, then pulled me into his. I'll wager that, on the scale of kiss-taste, a drag of Marlboro followed by a swig of Bud in a forbidden pool in the chlorinated dark still ranks pretty high.

—Through a chain-link. Soccer field. Drummer in a punk band.

—Curled around my firstborn's body, flesh-drunk, I kissed her chins and cheeks and tiny soft lips which parted, and for the briefest of moments we soul-kissed.

—I'd met the boy from the next town on my sixteenth birthday, in line at the DMV. He told me I was pretty and asked for my number. I'd never felt so grown up in my life. When he called, I said yes, so he picked me up and drove me to a lake with a boathouse. Once inside, he licked my face.

The next time he called I begged my sister to tell him I'd been sent to boarding school. She did, but charged me thirty minutes of back-scratching.

—Years before, my sister and I practiced on each other in a hotel bathroom. We also critiqued each other's "sexy walk." We never spoke of this again.

—After snowmobiling in Wisconsin. His lips were so chapped that they cracked mid-kiss and I swallowed his blood. I thought this should end up meaning more than it ended up meaning.

—Sitting on the fountain rim in Prague, I heard a commotion behind me. Before I could turn, something slicked the back of my neck—bird droppings?—and then the skinny back of a Romani ("Gypsies," I'd been warned by the Czechs, "all thieves") sprinted past, his hoot lingering after his boot soles flashed around the corner.

Was it a dare? An insult? Panicked flirtation? A distraction designed to remove my wallet from my bag? Here I sit, twice-my-life away, puckered, still responding to that kiss.

—The one with the girl. I kissed her not for her sake, or my own, but for the boys who were egging us on. Were I again presented with her soft lips, I'd do better.

—Strange that after all the lips, the censored kiss is the one I gave my daughter. Fourteen years ago I published a poem about it, which, the editor said, received some "interesting" feedback. Hate emails. All from women.

Recently, I found them. This time, they struck me as funny. Maybe, I thought—for so this world ripens us— maybe the women would, too.

—What's a kiss but two eels grappling in a cave of spit? Best not to overthink it.

—My grad school boyfriend had a mustache and beard. I didn't imagine I'd like them, but I did. I could kiss him for hours, the halo of scratchy hair making the central hot-soft even hot-softer.

But then came the month when we couldn't make rent, so he got a job delivering pizza, a spectacularly bad idea. Fayetteville's streets twisted around hills, and he had no sense of direction, so his pizzas were reliably late and cold. Tipping actually *was* just a city in China. Within three months he'd get rear-ended by a bozo without insurance. But I'm getting ahead of myself. What I wanted to tell you: drivers had to be clean-shaven. It was policy.

Before his first shift, he took a razor from its package. He entered the bathroom hirsute, and exited . . . wrong. I kissed him, and the kiss, too, was wrong. He slumped on the bed with his red, scraped jowls. "Wait a minute," I whispered, inspired, "I'll be right back." I took his razor and shaved "down there," shaved off every single hair. I thought it would be a turn-on, but I didn't feel sexy. Not at all. I looked like a child, like a Barbie. Now we were in it together, broke, depressed, slumped, razor-burned, and bald-jowled.

Reader, I married him.

—Today is our daughter's fifteenth birthday. These days, she and I rarely kiss.

—Maybe, at the end, there will be a reckoning of kisses. Maybe, along with good deeds, they tally our generosities of flesh. Maybe how we're judged is this: Were you a waste of breath? Maybe eternity feels like an endless kiss.

....

Tommy's parents wave from the porch as our minivan pulls up. His dad smiles, and that's when I see he's missing about half of his teeth.

Before retiring a few years back, Gerald was a mechanic. During high school, he'd apprenticed at his uncle's garage, then serviced army vehicles while stationed in Germany, then returned home and kept fixing cars. Worked "from can to can't," worked Saturdays, feeding himself into the maw of busted trucks in unairconditioned Alabama, feeding a wife and three kids. Eventually he'd own his own shop, Franklin Automotive. In addition to repairs, he had a line on "totals," wrecks the insurance company didn't consider worth fixing. Gerald considered otherwise. He'd buy two or three of the same model at salvage auction and Frankenstein them together. Technically he wasn't allowed to sell them—"branded title" and all that—but he figured there was no harm in it, as long as the customer knew. He loved to negotiate, and that man could sell an icebox to an Eskimo.

Twenty years before, I'd bought my first car from him, after Tommy and I were engaged. I drove it, a black Cherokee, for four years, but it was haunted. Before he cobbled it together, I'd made the mistake of wandering his scrap yard and discovered the salvaged Jeeps. I stepped over the witchgrass and peered into the badly front-ended wreck. Dangling from the spiderwebbed windshield, a clump of long blonde hair.

Gerald's body, eighty-two, is the one chassis he can't repair. Shingles, macular degeneration, hypertension, a spot on his kidney that needs watching, pneumonia, asthma, steroids for the asthma: so many small-parts failures. And now, the teeth. He stopped going to the dentist years ago. Finally got his rotten ones pulled. Gerald sighs as we lower ourselves into the living room's recliners. New teeth, he's been told, will set him back a pretty penny.

How much, we ask.

Sixteen thousand. He pauses. *Wish I knew how much use I'd get out of 'em.* He fiddles with his inhaler. *How much longer I'll be here below. How many meals I got left, you reckon?*

Tommy, Tommy's mom, and me: what can we do but shrug.

Don't need a full set, he says, addressing the ceiling, as if bargaining. As if God's scrap yard is lousy with spare teeth, all reasonable offers considered.

This, coming from a man who's worked six days a week for over sixty years: *All's I need's enough to chew a steak.*

I took a spectacular fall during a run, a real airborne wipeout that ended with a hard bounce and a gravel-spraying skid. I was pretty banged up, especially my left palm and my knees which were rivering blood down my shins, but nothing seemed broken. I limped home, grateful to find my husband there; he makes me braver. "It's nothing," I countered as he cooed and washed my wounds and dressed them in monster bandages.

My knees scabbed quickly, but I couldn't get the palm to heal, because, I assumed, I couldn't keep it rested and dry, what with the bodies of three children in my dominion. Finally it scabbed over in a thick, puckered star that itched and had a black lump. Gradually the star shrunk, until finally all that was left was this weird white blister, still black at the tip.

I waited for the blister to shrink, but it didn't. I waited for the black tip to fade, but it didn't. Although my palm didn't hurt—as long as I didn't applaud or do push-ups—it looked ugly. My youngest wouldn't hold my "bad hand" when we walked to pre-K. And after a while, I began to have the discomfiting feeling that the black thing was a foreign object beneath my skin. That my hand grew the white pillow to push away the black thing.

When I called Faculty Health and the nurse asked the reason for my appointment, I described my blister. She paused, then said, "Can you come in right away?"

I did, but the examining GP shook her head and said I'd have to see the hand surgeon in Jackson.

"A hand surgeon? Really? In Jackson? Really?"

She asked, "What days are you free this week?"

Now it was my turn to shake my head. "Couldn't we, just, you know . . ." I made a little fork-and-knife sawing motion.

"Hmm," she said. "Let me see if Dr. Yates is in the building."

"Shoot," Dr. Yates drawled, a few minutes later, palpating his fleshy thumbs around my palm, "We got this." He had me lie back and gave my hand a shot and then called loudly for his nurse to bring his "scalpel with the claws." Thus began the play-by-play that included "Almost got it" and "Whoopsie" and "Slippery little devil" and "You know, I started out as an English major." I could take the pain, but not the narration. I began to think I might pass out. Finally, after he said, "I'm just gonna rummage around in here until I nab it," I told him I was glad he was taking care of me but hoped he could continue silently.

He didn't speak again until he said, "Lookee here."

When I opened my eyes, he pointed to a surprisingly neat incision in my palm, like a slit for a dime. Proudly, he bandaged me, then handed me a plastic syringe. Inside its calibrated tube, the jagged piece of gravel.

I was glad my husband was home because I couldn't wait to show him. I held the syringe before his eyes, flicked it to make it rattle, and we laughed a little.

My husband said, "What are you going to do with it?"

"Do with it? I'm going to pitch it."

"I want it."

"You want it?"

"Yeah. I want it. I want to keep it. I'll put it in my office. It was in your hand for a month. It was a part of you."

I want to marry this man, I thought. I want to marry him right now.

But of course I already had, about nineteen years before.

ADDENDUM TO "SALVAGE"

Won a thousand dollars in a literary contest for one of these essays.

Bought my father-in-law a tooth.

NOTES

....

p. 23:   "Why I'm So Well Read" is for David Gavin.

p. 43:   "11. And I've Been Searching Ceaselessly For You Ever
          Since, Mon Amour" was written after listening to "Heavy
          Sleep" by pianist Bruce Levingston, and I dedicate it to him.

p. 90:   "When People Bemoan the Commodification of Art" is
          for Blair Hobbs.

p. 95:   "The Grief Vacation" is for Tom DeMarchi.

ACKNOWLEDGMENTS

APR: "Home Button," "I Come from a Long Line of Modest Achievers," "'If You Were Born Catholic, You'll Always Be Catholic,'" "I Knew a Woman," "Married Love," "Married Love, II," "Married Love, III," "Married Love, IV," "Returning from Spring Break, Junior Year at Notre Dame," "Still Have the Playbill," "When They Grow Up," and "Why I'm Switching Salons"

Arkansas International: "Another Missing Chapter in the Parenting Handbook," "Daughter, They'll Use Even Your Own Gaze to Wound You," and "My Father's Reminiscences"

Brevity: "Salvage" and "Some Childhood Dreams Really Do Come True"

Blackbird: "Safety Scissors" and "What I Learned in Grad School"

Creative Nonfiction: "I Survived the Blizzard of '79"

The Cincinnati Review: "Galore," "Mommy Wants a Glass of Chardonnay," and "Sweet Nothing"

Five Points: "Another Reason I Love My Mother," "Bad

Break," "What I Think About When Someone Uses 'Pussy' as a Synonym for 'Weak,'" and "Why I'm So Well Read"

Grist: "Nine Months in Madison"

Guernica: "A Reckoning of Kisses"

Gulf Coast: "Expiration Date," "I Was Not Going to Be Your Typical," "Low-Budget Car Dealership Commercial," and "Now I Glance Up the First Time They Call My Name"

The Kenyon Review Online: "11. And I've Been Searching Ceaselessly For You Ever Since, Mon Amour," "Our Friend the Memoirist," and "Pass the Vodka"

The Missouri Review: "The Grief Vacation," "Married Love, V," and "One Doesn't Always Wish to Converse on Airplanes"

Ninth Letter: *"Emulsionar"* and "The Neighbor, the Chickens, and the Flames"

The Oxford American: "Disharmony," "Proof," "Small Fry," "Small Talk at Evanston General," "The Visitation," "When People Bemoan the Commodification of Art," and "Your Turn"

The L.A. Review: "Goner"

The Normal School: "Orange-Shaped Hole"

The Southern Review: "Heating and Cooling"

"Goner" was the recipient of the Orlando Prize in Creative Nonfiction from A Room of Her Own. "What I Think About When Someone Uses 'Pussy' as a Synonym for Weak" was reprinted in *All We Can Hold: A Collec-*

tion of Poetry on Motherhood. "Some Childhood Dreams Really Do Come True" was reprinted in *First Encounters with One's Own Femininity.* My thanks to the Mississippi Arts Council for an Individual Artist Grant and the College of Liberal Arts at the University of Mississippi for a summer grant.

Ann Fisher-Wirth and Mary Miller both read this book in an early draft, and I thank them. Molly McCully Brown read several drafts, and our conversations and coffees shaped this book in many ways. Ivo Kamps, Chair of the English Department, makes possible things that appear otherwise. My colleagues and students at the University of Mississippi and friends in Oxford and at Square Books provided inspiration and encouragement.

Judith Weber, my agent, of SobelWeber fame, continues to provide wise and generous counsel. My editor, Jill Bialosky, has been a joy to work with. It's a pleasure to be in the good hands of the good folks at W. W. Norton— I'm talking about you Erin Sinesky Lovett, Nomi Victor, and Steve Colca. My former editor, Carol Houck Smith (1923–2008) spent her sixty-year publishing career at Norton, and her guiding spirit endures.

My mom, Mary Anna McNamara Malich, affirms me daily in many loving ways, as she has from the start, despite noting that "This book has a lot of penises, Beth Ann."